CANDLES,
MEDITATION,
AND HEALING

How do candle rituals work?

What do candles do? The answer is simple: candles do nothing except burn when lit. You are the one who makes extraordinary things manifest in your life and the life of others.

Something special happens in your consciousness when you are working with candles. Candles become powerful magical tools when you invite God-energy to flow through them. The candle flame becomes your connection to the divine.

About the Author

Charlene Whitaker is a professional astrologer and metaphysician. She uses this background in her work as a counselor, teacher, lecturer, and writer. She has been using astrology, tarot, palmistry, spiritual development, and psychic abilities actively for years as tools for helping others on the path to self-knowledge, personal growth, and enlightenment. In addition to teaching advanced astrology at the Carroll Righter Foundation in Hollywood, California, Charlene has participated in radio and television talk shows and has been featured in newspapers.

Charlene is the founder of Cosmic Academy of Metaphysical Arts in Canoga Park, California, and devotes herself full-time to counseling and teaching. Her teaching techniques have proven effective in years of classes with hundreds of graduating students.

Light Up Your Life with

CANDLES, MEDITATION, AND HEALING

Charlene Whitaker

2003
Llewellyn Worldwide
St. Paul, Minnesota 55164-0383

FIRST EDITION
Third printing, 2003

Cover design by Lisa Novak
Book editing and design by Astrid Sandell
Candle illustration by Carrie Westfall

Library of Congress Cataloging-in-Publication Data
Whitaker, Charlene.
   Light up your life with candles, meditation, and healing / Charlene Whitaker.
      —1st ed.
        p. cm.
   ISBN 1-56718-818-4
      1. Candles and lights. 2. Rites and ceremonies. I. Title: Candles, meditation, and healing. II. Title

   BF1623.C26 W45 2000
   133'.2—dc21   99-057929

Llewellyn Publications
A Division of Llewellyn Worldwide, Ltd.
P.O. Box 64383, Dept. K818-4
St. Paul, Minnesota 55164-0383
www.llewellyn.com

 Printed in the United States of America on recycled paper

To Write to the Author

If you wish to contact the author or would like more information about this book, please write to the author in care of Llewellyn Worldwide, and we will forward your request. Both the author and publisher appreciate hearing from you and learning of your enjoyment of this book and how it has helped you. Llewellyn Worldwide cannot guarantee that every letter written to the author will be answered, but all will be forwarded. Please write to:

Charlene Whitaker
℅ Llewellyn Worldwide
P.O. Box 64383, Dept. K818-4
St. Paul, MN 55164-0383, U.S.A

Please enclose a self-addressed, stamped envelope for reply or $1.00 to cover costs. If outside U.S.A., enclose international postal reply coupon.

For Llewellyn's free full-color catalog, write to New Worlds at the above address or call 1–877–NEW-WRLD

Contents

Introduction

It seems like every time the subject of candle burning comes up there is a lot of explaining to do—especially if the people around you are non-metaphysical, though even metaphysical students are confused at times. I remember my family whispering among themselves about what they thought I was doing. You know, "she is over there doing 'rituals' or something that might be strange or manipulative." Fear of the unknown should be a thing of the past as we move into the Age of Aquarius—a time of enlightenment. Now is the time to open yourself to the countless possibilities available to you through self-awareness.

Webster's Dictionary defines ritual as "a ceremonial act or action: any formal and customarily repeated act or series of acts." Ritual can be found in the methodology of almost anything we do. Most people have a basic ritual they use in mundane actions like taking a bath or brushing their teeth. *Ritual* is not a word to be feared.

When a candle "ritual" is performed, certain rules and methods are used. There is something special that happens in your consciousness, however, when you are working with candles. It is your time to work with God energy; it is a ceremony that holds a very special place in your heart. With candles, as with everything in life, there are different ways of doing things. Life is what you make it, and you can make yours very special, not just with candle rituals, but with everything that you accomplish.

I have been asked, "What do candles do?" The answer is simple, candles do nothing except burn when lit. You are the one who makes extraordinary things manifest in your life and the lives of others. The candles are only an extension of your consciousness, symbolic of persons, places, and things. It is when you ask that they represent something or someone in your life that they become very powerful, but only because you have asked that the God energy flow through them to assist you in your work as physical proof.

Some of us need more than prayer. I look for the answers to my prayers in the candles, and you can too.

The candles work based on the strength of your belief that what you are performing is valid. If you light a candle and walk away from it with no special blessing or need, then very little is produced. I don't believe that anyone can light a candle without some purpose in mind. When a candle is lit at dinner, even without a blessing or prayer, it still causes something to happen—if nothing else, it adds to the ambiance of the room. When you lit the candle on your table, somewhere in your consciousness you wanted to create love, romance, harmony, and balance. If all of that can be created without even trying, think what you can do if you light a candle and pray for something with all your heart!

Using an altar and doing candle rituals can be a difficult time of testing. I had a student come to me once and say, "I lit one but nothing happened." Remember that when doing candle work you are not God, but a servant and channel for God energy to flow through. It is not up to you when something should happen. Your role is to do the work with love in your heart, then "let go and let God." Things will not manifest according to your time frame, but in God's time. It is important that you do not set limitations.

In the Bible, God said, "Ask and you shall receive." That seems like such a simple statement, but people ignore it in their search for the big picture. Life is so simple, and that statement is more powerful than you can ever imagine. Why? Because you *do* get everything that you ask for.

Doing candle rituals is not incompatible with Christianity or other belief systems. When I use candles, I feel like I am taking the very best of all the religions I have studied and using them to help myself and others. Don't worry about what label you should put on your candle work. The only person you have to answer to is yourself, and that flame of light that is your connection with your Supreme

Being. Be a loving and giving person as you begin now to "light up your life," and all those who follow your light.

CREATING
YOUR INNER
SANCTUARY

When you are doing healing and spiritual work, you will first need a place to perform your rituals on an inner level—a place inside you given reality by creating a sanctuary with a beautiful natural environment.

The inner sanctuary is a must on your list of ritual paraphernalia. It will be used in conjunction with your creative visualizations, meditative work, and holistic healing to help yourself and others. This is not a place where you can take other people with you. It is a charged sphere within you, that place where God decided to hide out. We have been instructed to prepare an altar in our hearts, where there is a candle that burns constantly, and from that inner flame you can light other candles to help and heal. This is the master flame from which all other candles are lit.

Meditation:
Creating An Inner Sanctuary

To create your inner sanctuary, allow yourself to get very comfortable, perhaps in a reclining position. You should be free of pressures. Loosen your belt, unbutton the top button on your shirt, and get as relaxed as you possibly can.

Begin now by taking a deep breath in through your nose. Hold it for a few seconds, then release it slowly through your mouth. Feel your body go loose, and limp, and lazy. Let your jaw drop and remain very relaxed. Allow all of your muscles to relax. Let yourself go and become very tranquil and peaceful, very relaxed.

Imagine yourself in the most beautiful natural environment. Create this place in your mind. It can be a place you have been before, or you can create an environment that appeals to you—a forest, near a stream in the mountains, or a mountain top, beside the sea, in a meadow where there are all sorts of deer and rabbits, or a tropical paradise. It could even be as far away as another planet or the center of the universe. Whatever you have chosen, feel very comfortable and peaceful in this environment.

Now, explore where you are, and change anything you would like to make your sanctuary more home-like and comfortable. Just let your imagination go free and be a creator. You might want to cleanse the whole area with white light and then add golden light for the divine presence of God and for protection and safety. Perhaps you want to build a special building or shelter there. Remember, you only have to think the thought and it is done. Arrange things for your convenience and comfort. Next, select an area in this environment where you would like to build your altar. Just walk around until you begin to feel a very special vibration, and this will be the perfect and right place for your altar. Now allow your higher consciousness to guide you in arranging your inner altar. Don't doubt, just let go and let God.

Now that you have your altar, light a white light candle and place it in the center. This is for your protection and enlightenment, and it will never go out. Bless it in the name of the Father, the Son, and the Holy Spirit, or with Infinite Light and Energy. In the future, you will use the flame from this candle to light all other candles that you place on your inner altar.

From this moment on, this is your very own place to go whenever you desire. All you have to do is desire to be there, and you will be. Each time you return, you will always find the atmosphere very pleasant and harmonious. This has become your special place of power where you will always be a co-creator with God.

BUILDING
YOUR
MATERIAL ALTAR

Now that your inner spiritual altar has been created, it is time to create a place for your rituals and prayers here on the physical plane. Before attempting to create your altar on the physical plane, you should have worked with the energy of your inner plane for a while.

Once you are ready to create your material altar, your first step is to select a location in your home and consecrate it as a designated place where you are going to be in contact with God. Wherever you decide to create your altar, you can always be sure that the Infinite Energy of God will be there. The location should be cleansed—both with a good household cleaner and drenched with the White Light of God. You want to be sure that all previous vibrations that existed in the room are removed.

If at all possible, arrange your altar so that it is facing the west, so that when you are standing in front of it, you will be facing the east. This is optional.

Keep in mind when choosing your altar location that when you burn candles there is going to be some black smoke. This could cause damage to your furniture, especially the walls and drapes. You can expect to clean your drapes once every three to six months, depending on how much you actually use the altar. Also, the walls will need to be washed or repainted at least once a year. I have found that white walls are the best.

It is also advisable to have carpeting on the floor, as there will be times when you will want to lay on the floor in front of the altar to do your meditations. Wear house shoes or slip-on shoes so you can remove them easily, since you will be standing on spiritual ground once this place is consecrated. Therefore, if you are standing in your bare feet, the carpeting is practical and comfortable.

Next, select a cabinet or construct one of dark wood or wood that can be painted black to keep away all negative influences. If possible, it should have a drawer or cabinet space for storing incense, oils, candles, and other supplies for your rituals. Remember that candles are very heavy, especially those encased in glass, so build your cabinet to be very sturdy.

Once your cabinet or table is in place, spread a white altar cloth over it. An altar cloth is a white dresser scarf that you will use only for this purpose. Whether you make or purchase your altar cloth, it is advisable to have two or three of them so you will always have a clean one available. There will be times when you will want to change the altar cloth to remove the previous vibrations from a healing that you have done. Also, you can expect to spill candle wax from time to time, and the incense can become messy as well.

This white altar cloth is symbolic of the purity of our souls, and cleanliness is always acceptable in the sight of God. Do not use these cloths for any other purpose in your home and always launder them separate from your normal household items.

One of my students suggested that a large piece of glass cut to fit the top of the table might be a good idea. I agree wholeheartedly, as burning candles can be dangerous if one should break or be turned over. This panel of glass would be an excellent assurance of safety. Of course, put the white altar cloth under the glass if you choose this method.

A small altar is acceptable. You don't need to go wild and overdo things. It doesn't need to be four or five feet long. Use whatever is appropriate for your home and surroundings, but usually an altar a couple of feet long will be sufficient for doing most of your work.

Your altar will be a place where you will be doing healings, meditations, and prayer work. It is a very personal and private part of your life. Therefore, it is important to select a place where you know you will have privacy. If, for example, you put it in your living room, everyone who comes into your home is probably going to be curious enough to go over and examine it. When this happens, one of several things could occur: it may give the impression that you are practicing some sort of hooey-dooey stuff and you'll probably have to give an explanation of what you are actually doing, or the individual may touch or disturb the vibrations of something that you have on the altar and it will be necessary to cleanse it again. The bottom line is to keep your altar in a private place in your home.

ALTAR
EQUIPMENT

Keep in mind, as I am suggesting things for your altar, that no particular religious belief is being advocated. My suggestions consist of all of the very best qualities of many different religions. As you build your altar, you will be automatically drawn to certain items that make you happy and that are acceptable to your faith. For now, I am giving you basic guidelines from which to work. Remember, it is not the only way, so be open to change. After you have had your altar for a while, your inner guides will give you instructions about the arrangement of certain items.

In the center of your altar, you can place a small crucifix (symbol of sacrifice) or an equal-armed cross (symbol of the twenty-two Hebrew letters or alphabet as it has twenty-two different faces, it also represents growth and renewal, and perfect balance and atonement of the parts of man's being). Hang a holy picture or something that serves as a source of inspiration to you on the wall just behind the altar, if you'd like.

You may wish to put flowers or a living plant on the right side of your altar, as your spirit guides and masters love flowers.

Keep a white candle lit and burning at all times in the center toward the back of the altar. While it is a good idea to use the seven-day candles that are in glass for safety reasons, it is also more practical, since you will only have to light one about every six or seven days. Replace the white light candle each week with a new one, lighting your new candle from the old candle just before it is ready to go out.

The white light is symbolic of the light of God that surrounds you, Infinite Light and Energy, or the Father, Son, and Holy Spirit. This is the same light that comes from within you, that spark of God that is within everyone, and shared from your inner temple to the material temple. Therefore, always have one in both places. Keeping the flame going continuously is making a statement that you *are* the light and your life is filled with infinite energy to help and to heal.

Once you have lit the white light candle, use this flame to light all of the other candles on your altar. Doing this is like an extension of yourself and your God-consciousness to connect and attune you to the vibrations of the person for whom you are doing the ritual work for.

A bible or other spiritual book should be placed in front of the white candle. If you do not have any such book, then a book of inspiration is acceptable. Place something on your altar that you will read and that inspires and uplifts you, something that raises your level of consciousness. *A Course In Miracles,* by The Foundation for Inner Peace, has cards written up as daily inspirations or messages. This type of material is ideal for your daily verse. Don't put something there that you are not going to read, nor is it a good idea to read something that you give only lip service to—make it meaningful. It is good to start your daily prayers and meditation with an inspired thought.

Place a glass of water on each side of the white light candle. If possible, the glasses should be clear—you can use very special wine glasses or simple kitchen glasses, but choose something that is special to you. You will be using these for healing with holy water, which I will explain in a later chapter.

Next to the glass of water on the left side of the white light candle, place a small dish of salt. Salt is used for the purpose of cleansing any negative vibrations from entering your work area. Remember, you have to protect the people that you are working on as they are opened up to receive healings.

Place a candle snuffer on the left side of the altar. Do not extinguish your candles between your finger and thumb. If a snuffer is not available, cup your hand behind the flame and blow it out. As you do, ask that the blessing or healing continue on the spiritual realm. Raise your hands up into the air carrying the smoke with you. The smoke is like the continued energy of the candle's purpose.

The left side of your altar is the north, passive, feminine side. This is the side from which you receive energy. Therefore, place all candles and other objects on this side that you wish to be used as cleansing devices, or for all female things you want to work on.

The right side is the south side—the active, masculine energy. This is the side that you are working on, or where you are taking initiative and action in you life. The left side is for decrease, the right is for increase.

Therefore, consider that your altar is divided in half by the white light candle: and everything to it's left is the northern, feminine side, and everything on the right is the southern, masculine side.

PREPARING
YOURSELF TO USE
THE ALTAR

It is a good idea to take a spiritual bath before working at the altar. This is a bath that is taken for reasons other than cleansing your physical body of dirt or odor. You may want to take a regular bath first, if needed, to become physically clean. A spiritual bath is for attuning yourself to the higher levels of consciousness.

Draw a tub of water and put something in it to make it blue—such as a blue bath softener—some of your favorite oil, a few drops of disinfectant, and a few tablespoons of sea salt (or regular table salt) in the water. This is just one of many recipes that can be used for spiritual cleansing.

Soak in the tub for a few minutes, making sure that the water has completely covered your body. If a tub bath is not possible, then mix the same recipe (a weaker solution, of course) in a spray bottle, and use it to spray yourself as you take a shower. When you are finished with your bath or shower, put on a robe that will be used only for your spiritual altar work. Make this robe a very special one. It can be any color or type of fabric that you wish. As with your altar cloths, cleanse this separately from your regular laundry. Put on your special pair of slippers for your altar work.

If it is not possible for you to take a spiritual bath or shower, at least slip into your special robe before you do any of your altar work and wash your hands. The clothes that you wear on a daily basis become filled with the tensions and vibrations of whomever you have come in contact with.

NOW THAT
YOU HAVE
YOUR ALTAR

The possibilities are endless as to how you can use your altar. I'm sure you will think of many things other than what is covered in this book, but to get you started you can use any of the following suggestions.

Money

Place all cash and checks you receive in the center of the altar, just in front of your white light candle. Turn all of your cash face down. Bless the source from which it comes. Ask that this source—a person, a company—have an abundance of everything good in life and that what they gave out come back to them tenfold.

Ask that the money received be used to bring happiness, love, perfect health, prosperity, and abundance to whomever it goes to next. Finally, give thanks for having been used as a channel to help the people who will come in contact with the money, including yourself.

People

Place a picture of someone you know on the altar and light a candle near the picture or prop the picture up on the candle (only if it is in glass) and ask for this person to receive wealth, happiness, love, or whatever your particular blessing happens to be for.

Always end your prayers and affirmations for others with, "If it is God's will, so be it" or "If this is for the highest good of all concerned." With these words, you are always protected.

Your intent is not to manipulate anyone's life. Even if you are asking for something wonderful for that person, they might not want it. What you think is wonderful may not be what the person receiving the blessing thinks is wonderful. Therefore, always state one of the affirmations after each blessing and you won't be held karmically responsible for what takes place with that individual.

When you receive a card or letter from someone, you can place it on the altar and ask for a blessing in the same way that you did with the picture. Remember, if it is from a woman, put it on the left and from a man, on the right of your altar.

General Healing Prayers

Take a picture of a person to whom you are sending a healing and place a gemstone directly over the part of the body in the image that needs a healing. A herkimer diamond (double-terminated clear quartz) works exceptionally well because it has a point on each end. You simply place one point on the photo, covering the part of the body that needs healing, leaving other end open to receive or draw in energy.

A New Baby

You can perform this blessing at the time of the birth of a new baby and for the mother and father. Light your candles at the time labor first begins or as soon as you find out that it has begun, as this is the time it is most needed. Place a pink candle on the left side of the altar (feminine for mom), a blue candle on the right side (masculine for dad) and usually a white one in the middle for the baby. Mother and father on each side protects the baby in the middle.

The purpose of this is to send all of them energy for the big event—most people forget that the baby needs a tremendous amount of energy at this time also. It is fun to use taper candles for all three and observe how fast the candles burn and which symbols appear in them. This will keep you informed of the labor progress based on the way that the candles burn.

The candles on both sides give the baby the assurance that he or she is loved and protected from the very beginning of life. Of course, if the candles are not burning well, do some praying to send more light to whomever is in need.

Before Surgery

If someone you know is about to go into surgery, select a candle in the appropriate color (see pages 71–77) and light it a few hours before they actually go into surgery.

When I am asked to do a healing, I always fill out a blue index card. I write the name of the person who will receive the healing energy in the center of the card, and their affliction right below their name with brackets around it, which means to take away. For example, <gallstone surgery>. Also the date and time of their surgery, if applicable. In the lower left-hand corner (receiving side of card) write the name of the person requesting a healing for their loved one and the date that request was made. Then place the card right in front of the candle when it is burning.

Long after the candle has finished burning, I keep the card on my altar for further blessings and healing. You might consider using other colors of cards for different requests that you receive. For example, I use

Jane Smith
<gallstone surgery>
10/15/99

Jim Smith
10/4/99

A sample index card for a pre-surgery healing ritual

pink for someone desiring more love and compassion in their life, or green for more money, etc. Again, see pages 71–77 for more information on the significance of color.

Books

Anything that you are about to read should be blessed. When blessing books or any other reading material, I ask that only those things that God (superconscious mind) wishes me to hear be filtered through and that I become enlightened by the reading to help myself and others. If possible, and before you read it, place the book or reading material on the altar in front of the white light candle for a few hours or overnight.

To Cleanse and Purify

Place a large dish of sea salt on the left side of the altar to hold crystals that have been used for healings. This will cleanse and purify them for future use. Leave them in the salt for a few days or until you feel intuitively that they are ready to be removed. After cleansing, place them in the clean dish on the right side of the altar, ready for use in the future.

Water

The glass of water on each side of your white light candle is used for blessed water. You can use the following method to bless your water.

Fill the glass with regular tap water. Place the glass of water on the altar and put both of your hands over the top of the water and will healing energy into the water. Visualize the energy flowing into the top of your head, down through your arms and hands and into the water. Bless the water in the name of the Father, Son, and Holy Spirit, or you could say, "Bless this water with Infinite Light and Energy." At this time you will ask that the water be filled with all of the healing properties needed for the individual to whom you are sending energy and healing. Finally, place it back by the white light candle for a few hours or until bubbles form and then (if possible) the person it was prepared for should drink all of the water.

This blessing method is not only helpful and healing for you or someone else, but it is fascinating to watch the bubbles form. When the bubbles form, it means that the Holy Spirit has blessed the water.

Remember that if you are doing a healing for a woman place the glass on the left side and if it is for a man place it on the right side of the white light candle.

Prayer and Meditation

When I am doing my prayer work, meditations, and spiritual healings is when I go through all of the index cards that I have on the altar. Everyday at approximately the same time, I take each card in my hand and through prayer send more healing energy to that person.

When you do this, go through the entire stack of cards each day. If you agree to help to heal someone, take care of them, this means never forgetting even for one day to pray for them. If you adopted a pet would you neglect to feed and care for it? Or a child? Think about it, this is equally as important—it can't just be out of sight out of mind!

When you pray daily, never restate what healing you want done. Once you have lit a candle and invoked the light for this healing to take place, just *let go and let God*. To do otherwise would be like saying, "Hey God, are you sure you got that right?" Your desires are known, your daily prayer reinforces the healing energy or blessings. Always remember to humbly give thanks for the God energy that flows through you for the healings.

The length of time that you leave objects like cards, pictures, or money on the altar depends on what your higher guidance dictates to you. I always know when the energy stops flowing for a particular thing or person. When this happens, it means that the object is no longer needed and is my clue to take it off the altar.

When you are ready to dispose of the cards, create a special ritual by lighting a fire in the fireplace, and put the cards in the fireplace one by one. Ask that each person you have a card for go in peace as they are purified and cleansed of all negative vibrations, restored to perfect health and happiness. Bless them with Infinite Light and Energy one more time. Always give thanks.

SELECTING
A TIME FOR
CANDLE BURNING

There are many different ways you can determine the right time for lighting your candles. It depends on the type of ritual that you are doing. This can become extremely involved, so using some general guidelines are good enough. Don't go overboard.

New Moon

Candles can be lit after a new moon when it is waxing for matters in which you want to increase something, cause something to grow, to expand, enlarge, cultivate, germinate, or flourish. As the moon grows, so will whatever you are working on.

The new moon is effective for two weeks. A word of caution, however: do not light candles three days before the actual date of the new moon, as this time is called "the dark of the moon."

Full Moon

You can light candles after a full moon, when it is waning, for matters in which you wish decrease, reduction (weight), lessening, shortening, shrinking, or weakening. As the full moon wanes, diminishes, or dies off, so will the things you want to end.

Planets

Each planet and the sign that it rules can be used for further guidance. Even the time of the day is ruled by a certain planetary influence. I am an astrologer and could go into great detail with the meanings of the signs and planets for candle burning, but since there are so many wonderful astrology books that explain the meanings, I feel that it is not necessary to go to such depths here. However, a brief explanation will get you on the right course.

The list below includes the days of the week that correspond to the signs of the zodiac and their planetary rulers. Therefore, you might choose to burn your candles on the day of the week that is most appropriate to your astrological sign or for that of someone else.

Day of Week	Planet	Astrological Sign
Sunday	Sun	Leo
Monday	Moon	Cancer
Tuesday	Mars, Pluto	Aries, Scorpio
Wednesday	Mercury	Gemini, Virgo
Thursday	Jupiter, Neptune	Sagittarius, Pisces
Friday	Venus	Taurus, Libra
Saturday	Saturn, Uranus	Capricorn, Aquarius

LIGHTING
YOUR
CANDLES

Try to buy your candles from a location where you feel good vibrations, nothing dark and gloomy. It is a good idea to dress all of your candles when you first purchase them.

The first dressing of your candles should be done with an essential oil of your choice. Oils can be purchased for all of the different types of rituals that you wish to do, or you could create your own oils. I have one special oil that I bless all of my candles with when I first purchase them.

Anoint and bless your candles by saying out loud, "Bless this candle in the name of the Father, the Son, and the Holy Spirit," or, "Bless this candle with Infinite Light and Energy, so be it, and I give thanks."

When it is time to use your candle, anoint the candle again with the oil of choice for whatever you are working on.

The following diagrams show the directions for anointing the candles. Dip your index finger into the oil, then apply the oil to the candles. Each time you change directions, repeat the blessing.

Front of candle

Back of candle

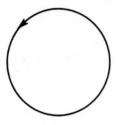

Top of candle

Wick of candle

THE WAY
YOUR CANDLE
BURNS

If the flame is very low, the energy around or running through the person or thing it was lit for will be very low. In fact, it may indicate that the person you are doing healing work on is not receiving the energy well. Conversely, if the flame is very high, the energy around you is very high, or the energy is being absorbed by the person receiving the healing or blessing. I always light a candle when I have any spiritual group meeting in my home and it's fascinating to watch how high the flame gets at times as the energy in the group increases. I started to realize this through observing the candle and my clients.

One particular spiritual healing stands out in my mind. I received a phone call from the husband of a very dear friend of mine. The husband, by the way, did not believe in "metaphysical mumbo jumbo" but was open to any assistance under the circumstances. My friend had just delivered a baby girl, and all three were at the hospital. She had encouraged her husband to call me to assist with a healing—thus the phone call from a frantic father.

He explained to me that their baby girl had just been born and was bleeding internally. Transfusions were being given, but the doctors didn't know if she could be saved. I told him not to worry, that it would be taken care of. This statement was the first step toward a successful healing because it was doing two things—first of all, there is great power in the spoken word and the affirmation put the father's mind at ease and gave him hope; second, I was convincing myself that all things are possible with God. The affirmation was stated in such a way that it led us both to believe that it would only be a matter of minutes before the condition would be resolved.

Next, I prepared a candle by blessing it for spiritual healing and lit it from my white light candle, using an incense stick. The candle was barely burning, so I knew the energy was not being received by the child. I went into the stillness and astrally projected to where the baby was in the hospital. Mentally, I made passes over the baby and cleansed her aura. I visualized her being totally encased in white light (symbolic of the White Light of God).

I willed powerful, spiritually healing energy into the child while holding a firm image of her being strong and healthy at the same time. I watched her for a few moments to see how she was accepting the energy and discovered that she was having difficulty breathing. I proceeded to create the same breathing rhythm for myself that the baby was experiencing. When we were both breathing the same, I gradually started to breathe normally, bringing her along with me. I continued until she began to breathe normally. However, I still did not sense the response I felt should be there and decided that I should talk to her. I told her that I loved her, that her mommy and daddy loved her, and that they wanted very much for her to stay, that they needed her. Then, with my mind, I placed pink light (which is for love) around the aura of the white light, and returned back from the astral projection.

When I opened my eyes I noticed that the flame on the candle was about two inches high, and I knew that the child was allowing the energy to flow through her and for the healing to take place.

That evening I received a phone call and was told that the bleeding had stopped and the baby was out of intensive care. During the following seven-day period, whenever I would pass the altar and see the candle, I would say out loud, "I love you, and I really care about you."

The candle allowed me to be in touch with the child long after the initial healing had started. The child is six years old now and a perfect picture of health.

Just an added note of interest to any astrological student: the secondary progressions in the horoscope are based on one day after birth equaling one year of life. Therefore each of those six days after her birth was having an influence on her life for the first six years of life. This little girl has always been extremely active and talkative. Her mother complains that she is too active at times. I have to laugh when I hear this, as during the first six days of her life she was being given a tremendous amount of energy by not only me, but also by her parents and everyone else who was praying for her to survive. A blessing in disguise, we always get what we ask for!

If you are burning seven-day candles in a glass container, there are so may fun things to watch for as they burn. All of the things that happen to the candle are a way of communicating to you what is taking place with the person, place, or thing you are working on.

If the flame makes the glass turn black, this is due to negative or low forces in and around the home or for whatever purpose you're burning the candle. If my white light candle starts to turn black, I go to my kids and ask, "All right you guys, what is going on?"

On the positive side, if this candle was lit for a healing on someone, then the black is symbolic of the diseased parts being dismissed from the individual. In this case, it is good to see the black. You should know that you are really helping that person.

If the candle flame burns black, it is important for you to extinguish the flame and take a damp cloth and clean the glass, then light the candle and bless it once again. Personally, I do not like to extinguish the flame once I have started the healing, so I wrap a wet cloth around a knife and clean the edges without putting out the flame. Some may consider this a little dangerous, so choose the method you feel most comfortable using, and do so at your own risk. Just clean it up! Continue to clean the candle every time it gets black until it burns clean—if you were a medical doctor you would clean a patients wound often. If you commit to doing something, go all the way.

As the seven-day candle burns down, some of the wax usually remains on the sides of the glass, forming all sorts of designs. Refer to the dictionary of symbols (beginning on page 115) for the individual meanings of the images that might form, and use the guidelines in the diagram below for reading the images.

Have an imaginary dividing line

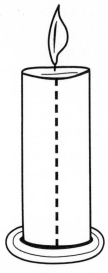

Something or someone else influencing your life

This is your personal message, as you are the creator

Something on each side can indicate an exchange of ideas or experiences with someone else

I never have to go to a counselor for guidance because I am given information daily from my white light candle. The symbols always seem to have a very significant meaning in my life, and it brings me pleasure to do readings on the candles. I have devoted a chapter in this book on the symbology of candle designs, so have fun in your discoveries. Some of the things I have seen in the candles have raised the hair on my head, and I feel blessed to have been receptive enough to know the meanings. The answers are always there for us, if we can just open our hearts to see them.

THINGS TO
REMEMBER

When you light candles for someone, you may want to write the name of the person for whom you are doing spiritual healing or blessing on a piece of paper and place it under the glass candle or candleholder. You might create an affirmation for that individual and place it under the candleholder or glass container. Sometimes it is more appropriate to write a prayer—for healing, wisdom, inspiration, et cetera—and place that under the candle. By placing the name and affirmation or prayer under the candle in writing, it is symbolic of pressing that message through the wax. As the candle then burns, the energy is constantly being reaffirmed.

Placing a mirror under the candle will amplify the energy. Just as mirrors are used to increase light they can be used to intensify the energy of the candle's purpose. Actually, the candle has no energy in itself, but its symbolic energy is what I am referring to here.

My students often ask questions about candle sizes. I don't really have any set rules for the different sizes that are available on today's market. Using a practical approach is usually the best way to select candles. If you are on a tight budget and can't afford to buy seven-day candles for someone, then a small four-hour votive will accomplish just as much.

After all, it's the thought that really counts. Therefore, purchase your candles according to what you can afford and by what brings you pleasure.

Follow your heart.

CANDLE
COLORS

Choosing the right colors for your candle rituals is important. You can make your selections from the colors listed on the following pages. Whenever you are in any doubt as to the proper color to use, always use white. If you do not have the color candle needed for your ritual, select the white glass candle and tie a ribbon around it in the color you need to burn. It's a good idea to have several extra white candles available. Also purchase and have available ribbons of every color for use, if needed.

There are entire books written on the subject of color, so I have only listed the colors below as guidelines to follow. If you get confused about the proper color to use in your rituals, listen to the voice that comes from within. Learn to follow the impressions that come to you through your meditations and prayers.

White

Symbolic of purity and innocence, purity of heart, simplicity. A desire to return to youthful times. Burn white candles when you want to just clean things up. Use as "The Christ Light," "The Light of God" that surrounds us. Burn at all times for truth, light, and protection. When you surround something with white light, you remain open to only the enlightenment of your higher consciousness. White light keeps the garbage out!

Red

This is the color of strength, vitality, physical desires, passion, and energy. Use red when you need a boost of energy, or if there is a need for you to take action and assert yourself by being more aggressive, outgoing, and ambitious. This is the color of God Power that flows through the universe and is present within us. Be careful with this power-driven color, it can create an imbalance if too much of it is consumed.

Pink

This warm color indicates joy, happiness, love, and affection. A certain weakness can be associated with pale pink, such as immaturity or someone who desires protection and a life where they are continually nourished. Burn a pink candle for delicate conditions in a love matter and at times when you need to be gentle, forgiving, kind, understanding, and affectionate. Of course, this is the color that attracts and enhances romance. Use pink when you desire to give your love or attract it into your life.

Orange

This is the color of creative expression, decision-making, ambition, and self-confidence. Use when you need that self-control in the way in which you express yourself. Orange brings in the qualities of optimism and fearlessness. Personally, I find this color difficult to burn as my mind just won't stop—orange makes me feel as though there is nothing too difficult intellectually. That's good of course, except when you want to sleep.

Yellow

With yellow you have the opportunity to activate strong mental energy, but with wisdom and imagination thrown in. Use yellow candles when you are searching for self-fulfillment through the inspirations received on a higher level of consciousness. This is a good color to use when you are searching for the answers to a problem, taking final exams, or when you need clear thinking. When you need to organize your thoughts and get your life in order. Use yellow to improve your mind and memory. For bright, happy people with an optimistic attitude for learning.

Green

This color is usually regarded as a favorite as it represents harmony, balance, abundance, prosperity, money, and success. Burn green candles when you desire change to bring new growth into the person's life. You must be prepared for the change. Money and success is possible here but you need to persevere. Green also has social implications.

Blue

Light a blue candle for spiritual understanding and divine healing. It brings in harmony, peace, and tranquillity. Since it has such a strong calming effect, you can project patience and understanding whenever needed. Use blue when affection and sentiment are needed. Provides a soothing, calming, sedating effect on the person you light it for. Blue cools a fever, for example, and helps a person to relax.

Lavender and Violet

A spiritual color that transmutes negativity and disharmony. Lavender and violet are strongly associated with mysticism, inspiration, intuition, idealism, and higher planes of existence. Improves your meditations. Enhances the dream state.

Brown

This color brings you back down to earth with its practicality and reliability. Use brown when you need to be productive and responsible in your work environment. It will assist you in getting grounded to the here and now. You may feel a strong sense of duty when using this color. Brown is an excellent color to use for business growth and productivity.

Multicolor (Rainbow)

If you're not sure whether you are using the right color, or don't know exactly what to ask for, then this is your solution. The rainbow candle has at least seven layers of different colors encased in a glass container. As the wax burns down, you are drawing in the energy of that particular color. I sometimes use it for a seven-day blessing, bringing into someone's life all of the individual energy colors.

CANDLE
READINGS

Votive Method

This is a type of candle reading or counseling technique that I created quite by accident, and it has proven to be very accurate and a bundle of fun. The beginning stages of this type of reading started when I used a tin pie pan and drew a zodiac wheel in the middle of it. I placed a votive candle in the center of the zodiac.

As the candle melts and burns down, base your reading on the houses of the zodiac that the wax flows into. Of course, this process takes several hours to do, and it should be done in the privacy of your own sanctuary. This is an excellent technique for things that you ask about yourself, but it takes quite a while to get the answers.

Let's take an example. Suppose you are scheduled to take a final exam in two weeks and are asking for assistance or guidance in taking the exam. You might choose a yellow candle, place it in the center of the wheel, light it from your white light candle, and place it on the left side of your altar—you want to *receive* information. When the candle has burned all the way down, you discover that most of the wax has fallen into the sixth house of the wheel. This is saying that you need to study and apply yourself on a daily basis and not save everything until the last minute to memorize. You also notice that part of the wax falls into the tenth house of the wheel. This implies that you will receive recognition and honors for your work—probably a very good grade.

Now let's try another example. A client calls and wants to know how a relationship will turn out. The candles can indicate how things are going at the present time, and where each of the two people are coming from. This time you will need two votives placed in the center of the wheel—one on the left (feminine) side for the woman and one on the right (male) side for the man. You can also place the candle signifying the younger person on the left and older person on

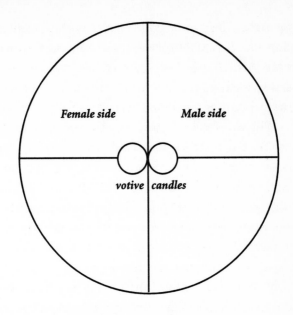

A sample reading using two candles

the right. This can be done for any type of relationship: love (to see if two people are compatible), marriage partners, boss/employee, child/parent, siblings, and so forth. Always put the most dominant person, the male, or the oldest on the right side of the wheel.

With two votives representing the two individuals, you'll need to check the candles regularly. A close observation of how the wax is melting is very important. First, observe how fast the candles are burning, whichever one starts to drip first indicates how active and enthusiastic the person is. Let us assume that two pink candles for lovers are being used, and the one on the left starts to melt into and toward the one on the right. We can determine from this that she brings love into his life. If his candle then melts in toward hers, he gives love back to her.

Then watch where the wax begins to flow onto the astrology wheel, the area of interest that each is moving toward. Let's assume that the wax falls into the fifth house of the wheel and curves around into the seventh house: *they start out as lovers, and the relationship eventually progresses into a marriage.*

That was an easy one. Let us assume that your client has asked, "Will we ever be lovers?" This time the wax drips differently. Suppose that the woman's candle wax flows into the first house and then into the second house: *she is pretty selfish, thinking of herself, and perhaps only interested in making money and having possessions at this time.*

Then you look at the man's wax and realize that it flows totally into the woman's side and into her first and second house: *he will make over and adore her, and will do everything he can to make her financially successful.* In addition, the wax drippings have formed an iceberg: *locked-up emotions, a great deal beneath the surface.*

My answer to the client would be, "Yes, you can become lovers, but be careful. Make sure that you come together for the right reasons. It seems as though you are pushing yourself onto her, doing everything to please only her. What is in this relation-ship for you? Are you willing to sacrifice your feelings and emotional needs just to be with her?" So, you see it becomes a one-sided relationship if it continues.

These readings are a lot of fun and very informa-tive. Be sure to remember when you are lighting can-dles for someone else that you always ask, "that it be for the highest good of all concerned, and only if you are meant to know, and if it be God's will, not yours." With this statement, you are in no way manipulating anyone else, or nosing into their privacy without per-mission—unless, of course, they personally give you permission. And by the way, if you are not meant to know, the message will be utter nonsense.

The symbols that form in the wax as it is burning can be very informative. It doesn't matter if the candle is a votive, cabala, taper, or candle encased in glass, you can read them all. The candles encased in glass seem to be the most fun to interpret, as there is always some kind of a scene being created as the candle burns. You will be looking at the residue of wax that remains on the sides of the glass as the candle burns down.

This is the type of reading that enables you to use many of your metaphysical talents all rolled into one. Since I use symbols in almost every type of reading that I do, they were easy to incorporate. Symbols are used in dream interpretation, astrology, numerology, and tea leaf readings. Tarot card interpretation is almost entirely based on the symbolic meanings.

Taper Drip Method

To use the taper drip method, gather the supplies you need for the reading. Then, in the center of a half-sheet of typing paper, draw a zodiac wheel (a small zodiac template would be useful). Assemble all of the different colors of candles that were listed in the previous chapter (pages 71–77). It would be to your advantage to use tapers for this method. It will be much easier for your clients to pick them up and hold them without getting burned from the wax. Place the candles in a basket or container of your choice.

If you are not an astrologer, have handy a brief description of the houses of the zodiac (one follows in this book on pages 97–98). If you are an astrologer, create another zodiac with the current transits for that day on a flat chart wheel (optional). You will also want to have a small white votive candle burning for the readings—first, it will be for the protection of the Light of God that surrounds you and your clients, and for purity of thought; second, it will serve as a light for all of the tapers lit by your clients.

Begin the reading by instructing your client to select a candle of their choice. Pay special attention to the color that is chosen. Use your candle color guide to assist you in determining where their needs lie. For example, if the client chooses blue, then the client is saying that there needs to be more understanding in their life. Peace, harmony, and tranquility needs to be applied to something or some area. Keep in mind that that color will set the overall tone for the reading and indicates why they have come to you for assistance.

Aries	♈
Taurus	♉
Gemini	♊
Cancer	♋
Leo	♌
Virgo	♍
Libra	♎
Scorpio	♏
Sagittarius	♐
Capricorn	♑
Aquarius	♒
Pisces	♓

Natural order of the zodiac

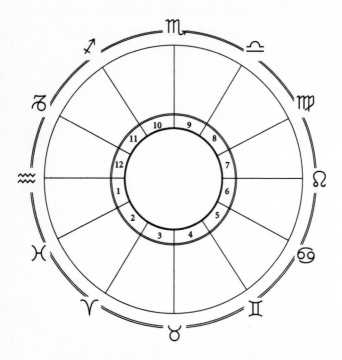

A sample zodiac wheel, based on an Aquarius sun sign

Next, as the client selects the color candle they would like to use, request that they give you their sun sign. Then place their sun sign on the first house of the horoscope wheel and each sign of the zodiac order around the remaining houses. Let us assume that Aquarius is the person's sun sign, then you would place the signs around the wheel as shown in the diagram on page 90.

Next pass the wheel to your client with the first house on the left side of the chart. Request that the candle chosen be lit from your white light votive candle. This symbolically links your energies with your client's. At this time you may use the eight of infinity to surround both of you with white light.

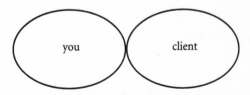

The Eight of Infinity

Each of you are then in a circle of white light for protection, and at the same time linked together to make it easier for you to connect with their consciousness. When the client leaves, just cut between the two circles (imaginary cutting) and the two of you then go your separate ways. The nice thing is that when your client leaves, you have given a gift of white light protection for them in addition to their fun and informative reading.

The next step is to instruct your client to allow the wax to drip onto the zodiac wherever they would like for it to drop. Encourage them to be the creators of their life. Some will let the wax go all over the paper, inside and outside of the zodiac wheel. Others will confine the wax to a small area within the wheel. It doesn't matter how they do it, let them use free expression. It allows them to feel that they are in control of the situation. Have them drip the candle wax for about one minute or less. As they are dripping the wax onto the paper, observe their actions and body language.

1. Is your client timid and shy? If so, this is a very sensitive person and you should treat them with sincerity and respect. You should respect all your clients, but be especially careful about joking around.

2. Is there great caution not to make a mistake and a sincere desire to follow your instructions carefully? This is an insecure person who doesn't feel comfortable with their own independent actions; a perfectionist, who prefers to follow the instructions of others.

3. Does your client spill wax on the table and all over the paper, not caring where it falls? This is your adventurer who enjoys a game of chance. Someone who faces life's challenges with courage. This person may not care who is in the way as they charge forward in life.

4. Does your client carefully drip wax into each and every house in the zodiac wheel? This one

doesn't leave anything out. An investigative mind that can handle intense situations under which others might break. Likes things that involve research, detail, and analysis. Many interests.

5. Is your client very careful to make all of the wax fall into just one concentrated area of the wheel? Here we have someone who can focus their attention with great drive and determination. This person will be the one to get the job done. May also be stubborn and locked into his or her own way of thinking.

6. Does your client close their eyes and let the wax drip anywhere? Led by blind faith. Encourage positive direction in life with a plan for how to do it. This is the type that stays home and watches television until the electricity is turned off. Doesn't worry about tomorrow because God will provide, which means that they don't have to do anything.

These are all first indicators of this person's personality and character. These are only a few examples, and neither you nor your clients can be limited to these reactions or explanations. Also if your client is like example six, don't respond by saying "you're a bum." You might instead say, "You really operate through faith, don't you?" Observe all of your client's actions, they tell so much.

Note: I've had more than one client choose two separate candles to work with. This is perfectly okay. Allow them to express their needs. Continue to pay close attention to the colors that are chosen. More than one candle conveys a great deal of versatility and creative qualities associated with these clients. This person is individualistic and doesn't accept limitations. A free thinker who dares to be different. The entrepreneur.

After one minute has passed, ask the client to blow out the candle and pass the wheel to you. Now that you have the finished masterpiece in front of you and you are excited to begin your interpretation, examine the wax for a few seconds to see if it forms any particular symbol (see the dictionary of symbols, beginning on page 115). Let's assume that you saw a butterfly. This would indicate freedom from whatever house(s) it falls into—a special blessing in life and, therefore, freedom. You would then discuss the symbol with your client.

Determine the meanings of the houses in the zodiac from the list on pages 97–98. For our example, I will use the fifth and sixth houses, assuming that the wax has fallen in this basic area, and combining the butterfly meaning. You might say, "You have been blessed and should be feeling greater freedom (butterfly) with your children, a creative project or romantic partner (fifth house) that could improve your health and work environment (sixth house)." Hopefully, you will be psychically attuned to be able to narrow down some of the possible choices of these two houses.

Houses of the Zodiac

House One: The part of your personality projected to others, vitality and life force, appearance.

House Two: Your financial condition, possessions, ambition, what you value.

House Three: What stimulates your mind, how and what you communicate, basic education, siblings, transportation.

House Four: What is happening in your home, how things end, the most passive parent.

House Five: How you are expressing yourself creatively, amusement and entertainment, love affairs, speculation, children.

House Six: Your health, diet, fitness, work environment and coworkers, service, efficiency.

House Seven: Your relationship with your mate, open competition, justice, fairness.

House Eight: Joint resources, financial security, death and transformation, sexual encounters, taxes, insurance, credit.

House Nine: Your own philosophies, higher education, religion, foreigners, long-distance travel, lawsuits.

House Ten: What is happening in your career, reputation, self-esteem. Most dominant parent.

House Eleven: Your hopes wishes and aspirations, groups and organizations, relationships with friends.

House Twelve: Things that are hidden or secretive, seclusion, institutions, spiritual service, karmic situations.

Now put together everything that you have observed. In the beginning of the reading, your client chose a blue candle, let's assume that this person let the wax drip in one specific place in the chart very carefully—it formed a butterfly that fell into the fifth and sixth houses of the zodiac wheel. You would begin your reading by saying:

> You are in search of spiritual understanding and guidance in your life, and it would be good if you could receive this inspiration in a way that is harmonious (blue candle).

> You probably take a practical approach toward the things that you do and are very careful not to harm anyone in your process of spiritual growth. It would be good if you always knew what is expected of you ahead of time in order to carefully prepare yourself (deliberate method of placing the wax on the wheel). It would be good if you could break away from this rigidity (butterfly) in the areas of your life that have to do with romance and creativity (fifth house).

> If you can permit yourself to change (butterfly) harmoniously (blue candle), you will be a more productive person in your work environment and feel healthier (sixth house). If

your work environment requires you to do a routine job without the ability to express your creativity (fifth and sixth houses), you may be setting yourself up for a situation that causes mental and physical stagnation.

At this point, continue your consultation based on the elements that you have to work with. In the first example, I selected an Aquarius sun sign. If you refer to this example, you will notice that the signs Gemini and Cancer are located on the fifth and sixth houses. You could then blend the qualities of these two signs by stating:

It looks as though you have a vast amount of creative talent and could be very versatile in your workplace. These talents can be administered in a leadership capacity which should appeal to you. Do you enjoy taking care of others in a nurturing way (Cancer)?

The next part of the reading is optional—it really depends on how much knowledge you have about astrology. If you are familiar with transits, then you can use them to determine when the activities will be stirred up that you have made reference to. As an example, assume that Mars by transit was moving through this sector of the chart. Mars gets things moving and creates a lot of activity wherever it is transiting in the zodiac. Therefore, if our pretend client does not start moving toward manifesting these changes in his or her life, then Mars will bring in some outside influence or person who will motivate and move them into taking action.

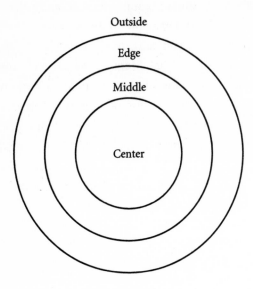

The zones of the wheel

What you must consider next are all the possible ways that the wax can fall into the wheel.

Center: If the wax falls in the center, then your client has always had this ability innate within them. It will seem like second nature or easy for them to do. They already have this operating in their life.

Middle: This is probably a quality or attribute that your client is working on manifesting in their life now. They know something about it, but they are not comfortable and confident yet. Learning stage.

Edge or Outside: In this instance, it will be something that is coming into your client's life that they are not yet aware of. Therefore, it will almost always be something new and quite possibly something they never considered. The farther out the drip is located, the greater amount of time until it becomes a part of their life.

Observe whether the wax falls on a house cusp. The house cusps are the lines that define the little pie-shaped segments of the wheel. It is like the door that opens into a room or house. The cusp opens into the house going in a counterclockwise direction.

Reading A

In this example, notice that the wax appears to have just left the eighth house and is operating fully in the ninth house. Your client would have just finished off some lessons of the eighth house and would be working on something in the ninth. Since it is on or near the outside edge of the wheel, it is something new. This client might have just been given finances (eighth house) to begin their higher education (ninth house) in a new field (outer edge).

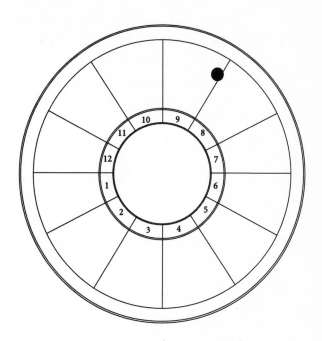

Location of wax dripping for reading A

Reading B

Here we have something that has been applied for (middle) coming into this person's life and it may mean quitting an old work environment (sixth house) for a new one. Since it is approaching the seventh house, we could say that the new work environment might be much more social and the competition might be greater (seventh house). Note: When doing a reading, assume that all drops of wax are moving in a counterclockwise direction.

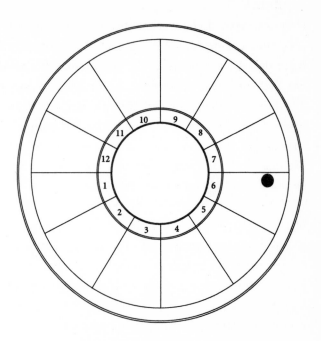

Location of wax dripping for reading B

Reading C

First of all, you can be sure that this is something that the person can do very well as it is located in the center of the wheel. As a matter of fact, it indicates a talent that was up to this point in the subconscious mind or it might have been an unrecognized talent (twelfth house). Since it is now in the first house, it should be a very obvious and a distinct part of their personality. Other people are aware of the talents, even if it is not obvious to the client (first house).

If there is more than one drop of wax in any one place, then it becomes more important and has greater impact on your client's life. If there were two drops of wax side by side in example A, it might indicate two things that they were planning to study in higher education. Or, if one dot of wax was in the ninth house near the center, you might say, "You are using the knowledge of something that you know very well to help you tackle this new subject." Or, "What you already know will be the foundation for your new subject matter."

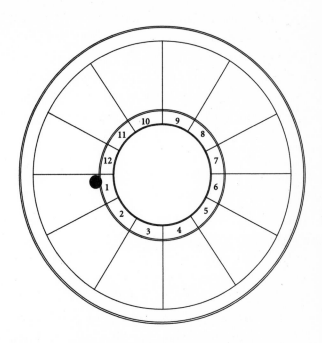

Location of wax dripping for reading C

BRINGING
THE MAGIC
TOGETHER

If you light candles for someone else and you discuss their life, remember that you are not making decisions for another person. You can show them the different options they have, and build their confidence to enable them to make their own decisions based on the guidance and counseling you have provided. Please, resist telling people what to do with their lives.

Burning candles demonstrates that whatever you strongly desire for yourself or another will manifest. The impressions that come through symbols in the candles remind us of the continuous progress and finally the successful results of what the power of the mind can do.

Use your candles as powerful fuel to bring in God energy to dramatically improve your life and the lives of others. As you explore the possibilities through the magic of candles, may you be blessed for your loving gifts to mankind. Best wishes to all who follow and use the "light."

DICTIONARY
OF
SYMBOLS

A

Acorn: A seed has been planted within you to create great opportunities for growth.

Airplane: An awakening spiritually. If the plane is positioned up and climbing, then you are soaring to new heights. If it is in a descending position, you are backsliding.

Alligator: Tremendous verbal power. Don't get carried away by fears that surface from the subconscious mind.

Anchor: Something or someone is holding you firmly in place. A deep emotional passion with which you feel secure and comfortable.

Angel: This is one of God's messengers. You are being protected spiritually. A very favorable symbol. Be still and listen for the next few days.

Ant: Perseverance; you can drive relentlessly forward. You are able to carry a heavy burden. This is a time in your life when you can be industrious and organized.

Arrow: Take swift action now, something is about to be finalized. This can be the "arrows of love."

Astrology: Examine your relationship with life now. Consider a consultation for inner direction. Discover your view of the universe.

Apple: Are you feeling whole, happy, and successful? Usually associated with understanding and knowledge; therefore, if there is a bite taken out of it, you are obtaining that knowledge, feeding yourself that wisdom.

Ape: A large primitive life form, wild and untamed, with tremendous strength. Check your actions; are you falling into patterns of an uncouth person?

Archer: Direct your energies now toward your goals. You can see the direction needed.

Atom Bomb: A destructive force unleashed. You may have to deal with emotional explosions. Seek balance and harmony.

Attic: You have high ideals. Your higher spiritual self is being developed. You are drawing from a higher source of inspiration.

B

Baby: You are ready to give birth to a new idea or new beginning. Possibilities are promising, but remember to nurture your new project.

Bag: Are you left holding the bag? Contain your thoughts wisely.

Ball: You may be experiencing a lot of ups and downs in your life, but you have the ability to bounce back. The ball is in your court now.

Balloon: A feeling of being on top of the world soaring to new heights.

Banana: Phallic symbol. Possibly a need for more potassium in your body.

Banner: Success and recognition are yours now. Victory.

Bars: Who is going to jail? Your choices are limited. Do you feel boxed in or trapped?

Basket: Harvest time, symbol of abundance. Rewards coming your way.

Bat: Seeing through things clairvoyantly. Living too much in your subconscious mind.

Bear: A powerful attack may be coming your way that is unexpected. Reinforce your white light shield often. Don't enter another person's protected territory.

Beard: You appear to have great wisdom and can guide others now with maturity and responsibility. Make sure you aren't hiding behind something.

Bed: Escape into the subconscious. Sexual intimacy. Returning to a place where you feel safe and protected.

Bee: "Busy as a bee" gathering things of value into your life through hard work and determination. Everyone working together to accomplish a common goal.

Bell: Be on guard for a signal, message, or awakening that is coming. Usually favorable, fortunate news. If you see two bells, a marriage is in the making.

Bible: It is possible to attain spiritual knowledge through study and application.

Birds: Messengers. Spiritual freedom from anything on the physical plane of existence. Inspired thoughts and ideas are surfacing. If a dove, this is a very good sign, a blessing.

Bird Nest: The security of the family. If there are eggs in the nest, they would represent children. If the nest is broken, the home could be breaking up. Could the children be moving from the nest?

Boat: Are you embarking on an emotional journey? Be careful that you are not the one rocking this emotional boat. Passage away from difficult times.

Book: Your life is an open book. You are receiving recognition from others for your knowledge. Be especially aware of the lessons that come your way in the future.

Boot: Your firm foundation may be slipping away. Be careful that you don't get booted out of your position.

Bottle: Let the genie out of the bottle. Take the cap off and let the inspirations flow. You have had something bottled up for too long.

Bow: Put the finishing touches to your project. A surprise awaits you.

Box: Do you feel boxed in now or trapped?

Bricks: Building new cornerstones in your life. A new foundation that is long lasting and has great strength.

Bridge: This is a chance to take the shortest route to success. Crossing over the difficulties. The bridge that closes the gap between two souls.

Broom: It's time to clean up your act. Make a fresh new start, a clean sweep of things.

Bubble: See balloon.

Butterfly: Freedom from anything that holds you back. A blessing to come. Rising above the animal state to soar into your higher consciousness. If you allow the right amount of time for something to process, them something wonderful occurs.

C

Cage: Feeling as though you are trapped or confined. There needs to be more freedom in your life. The limitations may be imaginary.

Cake: Now you can have your cake and eat it too. Celebrate, and enjoy yourself.

Candle: The light of your life. Inspirations from above. You are shining the light for others with your wisdom and knowledge. Do you see the light?

Cane: Receiving support from something or someone. Who are you leaning on?

Canoe: Balance your life now by bringing in more harmony.

Car: Your efforts are getting you closer to your goals. Keep driving relentlessly forward. Where are you traveling?

Cat: Associated with the feminine part of self. Cats sneak about and can see in the dark. Someone may be doing something behind your back.

Cave: Entrance into the unknown or inner life. Tap into the subconscious now to find your strength through superconsciousness. This is an opportunity to delve into past things that need resolving.

Chair: Slow down and rest yourself. Your position or status is important. Sit up straight and listen.

Chariot: Patience and self-control. This is not driven by an engine; it is driven by your own power of concentration.

Circle: Without beginning and end, therefore infinite. Completeness. What goes around comes around. Possible marriage.

Clock: Time is on your side. It is time to get moving and stop procrastinating. Pay close attention to the numbers on the clock, and add them up numerologically. If it is 12 noon, then add 1 + 2 = 3. It could mean that at this particular time of the day something important could happen or it could equal a day of the month, et cetera—make a note of it. It could even be the twelfth month and the third day into the month.

Clouds: Stormy weather is on the way. A possible emotional downpour. If the clouds are light, good news is on the way; if dark, difficulty with something that may be upsetting.

Clover: Good luck and good fortune. A winner. Something magical is about to happen.

Coin: Watch your prosperity consciousness. Changes in your affairs.

Comet: Someone is coming in swiftly. An incredible new awakening. A tremendous amount of creative inspiration.

Crab: Protection from outside influences is easy to attain. Don't hold on too tight. Don't be a crab.

Crescent: New beginnings, increase, and success. Receiving something that has an emotional impact on you.

Cross: You may have a cross to bear. Equal-armed cross, perfect balance between the male and female parts. It is your choice if you go through suffering and sacrifice.

Crown: Attainment of your desires. Receiving success, recognition, and honors that you deserve.

Cup: If the cup is full (all wax), then your plans are filled with new hope and promise of the good things in life. You may receive a gift cup of rewards. If the cup is empty (when you can see through the wax), you may be cutting yourself off from the life force and from obtaining what is rightfully yours.

Cupid: This is always a symbol of love. Experiencing the harmony and bliss of a love relationship in it's early stages of innocence.

D

Daisy: Don't be too extravagant in any of your endeavors at this time. Keep it simple.

Deer: A beautiful, sensitive animal. Now you must deal with the gentle part of self that sometimes gets hurt.

Diamond: This intensifies and activates what is within. Find that perfection within yourself.

Dog: A loyal, trustworthy friend. If teeth are shown, someone you felt you could trust may be turning on you or attacking.

Dolphin: Leaping potential for abundance.

Dove: You are surrounded by peace and love. A time of spiritual awakening and blessings.

Drum: Get with the rhythm of this beat and begin to communicate or give out your messages. Be alert and listen to what is not being said.

Duck: When you see a duck in your candle, it signifies good luck. Happy family unity. Things are just "ducky" now!

E

Eagle: It is possible to gain through honors and recognition in your career. You can soar above any obstacle due to your great spiritual strength. There is a feeling of being uplifted and free from worry. You are capable of foresight and good judgment. You may be receiving something in the mail from the government.

Ear: Listen to what is not being said. There may be gossip about you. Are you paying attention?

Egg: An egg is symbolic of things that can be created. The beginning of a new life. Something that can develop and grow. Prosperity and abundance.

Elephant: Your strength and confidence is seen in your career. You may be elevated or promoted to a higher position. Just don't get into a big hurry, as things will progress slowly. A time when information is processed gradually, but you have the ability to retain what is studied.

Escalator: It will be quick and easy for you to arrive at your destination.

Eye: Awareness, intuition, and psychic abilities are yours now. You are seeing things clearly?

F

Face: Usually the face will remind you of someone that you know. This person will cross your path soon, or there will be an opportunity to communicate openly.

Fairy: The materialization of your fondest wishes. Mischief is in the making. This is a nature spirit, which is helpful and fun to have around.

Fan: Are you hiding or concealing something? Are you being mysterious?

Feather: Recognition for an accomplishment. "A feather in your cap." To Native Americans, when you are given a feather, it is symbolic of some courageous thing that you have accomplished.

Fence: This represents Mother Nature's boundaries. You may be experiencing limitations and restriction which make it difficult to move forward. Are you sitting on the fence not making an important decision?

Fish: There may be something "fishy" going on. This is usually a fortunate symbol. Since fish are prolific, things sprout and grow, therefore gain and abundance is evident.

Flag: An increase in material wealth. Victory, something to celebrate.

Fox: Are you jumping from one thing to another? There isn't enough concentrated effort directed toward your undertaking. Scattered energy. Transform yourself out of this dilemma into a situation that is much more positive.

G

Garland: There are honors coming to you through your achievements.

Gate: The gate is open, so move ahead with your plans. There is a new opportunity awaiting you.

Giant: There is a person with extraordinary powers who will have an incredible influence on your life. Has a situation grown to giant proportions?

Glass: Seeing things clearly. Thoughts can be assimilated easily.

Grapes: Enjoy the wine of life and nurture the spirit. You show great ambition and can bring your ideas to fruition.

Guitar: Life can be happy and harmonious when you are "tuned in."

Gun: Phallic symbol. There may be quarrels, danger, even the possibility of an assault.

H

Halo: Your inner light is showing. Tonight your lights are on bright!

Hammer: Power-building capacity. There is an opportunity to build new cornerstones in your life. Are you driving your point home?

Hammock: It's time to kick back, rest, and relax.

Hand: If the hand is open, your feelings are out in the open, you are extending yourself. If the hand is closed, keep your feelings under control. Give a helping hand. This may be the "Hand of God."

Hat: The different roles you play in life. Occupations.

Handcuff: Bondage. Not free to express yourself. Your hands may be tied in this issue.

Heart: Affairs of the heart, involving love, emotion, sympathy, affection, and feelings. Note the condition of the heart in the candle.

Honeycomb: Create a place in your life that contains the things that you treasure. An abundance of wealth is at your fingertips.

Horoscope: Get in touch with your destiny and purpose in life. You can be provided with a road map or plan to follow.

Horse: Great power and energy is available. Succumbing to an overpowering sexual appeal or desire. A wild and free spirit.

Horseshoe: Good luck and prosperity.

House: A symbol of self. Different stories in the house represent the different levels of consciousness. The basement is the subconscious mind; the main floor, the conscious mind; the top floor or attic, the superconscious mind. Which level are you receiving from?

I

Iceberg: You may be holding on to emotions that have been locked up for years. There is a great deal that must be exposed, which has been hidden beneath the surface of awareness.

Indian: Spiritual values and knowledge that can be received from your teacher (higher self).

Initials: Always refers to someone in your life.

Iris: A promise manifesting in your environment.

Iron: You are ironing out your problems with smooth sailing?

Island: An enjoyable retreat and place of relaxation, located in your consciousness, previously cut off by your emotions. Have you isolated yourself from others?

J

Joker: The ability to conform to any situation, when necessary. You are not being serious enough. Quit fooling around.

Juggler: This is the opportunity to apply many of your talents all at once and remain calm and in balance. Time is not on your side, so act quickly.

K

Kettle: What ya got "cookin'?" There could be a heated argument, but you have the ability to release the tension and end it quickly.

Key: There will be doors opening for you. Use this time in your life to obtain greater wisdom and knowledge.

King: There is a greater awareness of inner power and self-worth. Who are your values ruled by? You have the advantage now, become the master of your own world.

Kite: Something you didn't think was possible can be brought to fruition at this time. Great joy and success are yours in speculative matters.

Knife: There may be an abrupt separation, due to an argument. Keep in mind that a separation is not always sorrowful. This can be a time to cut out all the deadwood in your life.

Knot: Stress and anxiety may be high now. Your feelings are tied up and closed off. Bound to a situation that needs to be released.

L

Lace: Things are going your way. Love and financial gains are in the air. Surround yourself with exquisite things.

Ladder: Allow yourself to rise above the issue and just let go. Reaching new heights through advancement, promotion, or spiritual awareness.

Lamb: Express innocence and purity of thought. Be as gentle as a lamb.

Leaves: Lessons you have learned and methods to creatively express them. Things you have brought to a completion.

Leg: Things that have been relied on in the past will continue to support you. Don't be afraid to take that first step toward manifesting what you want in your life.

Letter: You have the ability to express and communicate with confidence. You may be receiving an important message about yourself. It doesn't have to come from a source you are familiar with.

Lighthouse: The Christ within shining through to assist and guide others along the pathway. Now you are "seeing the light."

Lion: Making a strong and courageous attempt to face anger and fears in yourself as well as others around you.

Lock: There are problems and emotions that are locked inside you. A friend or companion may be the key to releasing this issue.

M

Man: There is a part of you that is ready to initiate action that can be aggressive.

Map: Guidance and direction is needed. Your teacher can guide you through any obstacle along the pathway, reach out and ask.

Mask: Don't deceive yourself by the many different faces you wear. Be careful, things aren't what they seem. Look within.

Maypole: A sign of fertility. Your creative abilities are coming to fruition. There can be great joy and pleasurable times through an event forthcoming. You have earned a celebration for abundance.

Mermaid: You may experience a gigantic temptation to be with a seductive person.

Monkey: Play, have fun, bring immense happiness into your space. "Monkey around."

Moon: You are struck by love and romance. Feel confident in your expression, as you are divinely inspired. Write some poetry, get in touch with your subconscious thoughts.

Mountains: You can achieve a higher level of inspiration. Becoming aware of the spirit within.

Mouse: Timidity. Is there something gnawing away at you?

Mushroom: There is rapid growth and expansion of your psychic powers through your awareness and sensitivity.

Musical Note: Experiencing harmony and peace within. Happiness and good luck.

N

Nail: Are you receiving the strength and support you need from others? Don't allow things to slip away from you. Keep it together. What are you hooked on?

Needle: Now is the time to sew things up and finish a project you have been working on. You can receive recognition for your accomplishments.

Numbers: 1. Oneness with God. New beginnings with an enterprising attitude. It's time to start something and lead the way. **2.** Patience and cooperation are needed now. Be diplomatic in all your relationships at this time. **3.** Express yourself now with optimism and friendliness. **4.** Get grounded to the here-and-now by organizing yourself in a practical method. You will have opportunities to create new foundations that are well balanced. **5.** Express yourself creatively. Don't be afraid to try new things. Do things that are entertaining and fun. **6.** Become the comforter for your family and friends through service and duty. Give, give, give! **7.** Take a break, and be still and listen to that still small voice within you. Analyze your thoughts, letting go of the ones that you longer need. **8.** Put on that smart-looking suit and allow the executive ability go to work to capitalize on all of your hard work with good management. **9.** A time of completion. Forgive, forget, let go, and let God.

Nut: Your seed ideas have good potential for future growth.

O

Oak Tree: You can use incredible strength and perseverance. You are protected in your endeavors.

Oar: Steer and control your emotions on a positive course.

Octopus: Entanglement. Don't live in fear of an emotional trauma.

Owl: Subconscious awareness. Now you have the wisdom to recognize the hidden parts of self.

Ox: This is a fortunate time period, satisfying your earthly pleasures and desires.

Oyster: You can rise above your restrictions and limitations. It's time for your coming out party.

P

Padlock: See lock.

Path: What is your direction in life? Is the pathway clear?

Peacock: Possible fame and recognition. A time when you are filled with pride.

Pendulum: Stop jumping from one thing to another. Bring things back to normal; get back into a routine. Get back into the "swing" of things.

Piano: A wonderful symbol of creative expression.

Pot: What are you receiving that is nourishing and fulfilling?

Pyramid: You have mystical power and occult knowledge. You have gone through your initiation, and will be rewarded by good fortune.

Q

Quartz: Your energy level is high. Since you are a conductor of energy, use it to heal yourself and others in need.

Queen: There is a powerful woman coming in, whose influence is very helpful.

Question Mark: Hesitancy to move forward. Wondering if something is needed.

R

Rabbit: Your sexual desire is strong. You can produce through your innovative ideas. Be productive.

Rainbow: A sign of promise and balance for the future. Follow your dreams.

Rat: Treachery or betrayal from someone. Is something gnawing at you?

Raven: A sense of loss or bad news. A crippling fear of the unknown or death.

Razor: Cutting through all of the nonsense with sharp mental alertness. Getting things done.

Ring: Bringing something to a completion. A union without a beginning or an end.

Rose: The gift of love and beauty smells sweet and fills your heart.

S

Saddle: Don't allow yourself to be saddled with other people's problems. A possible journey in the near future.

Scales: Balance and harmony in the midst of change.

Scarab: Eternal life with the continual renewal of the things around you. Experiencing a spiritual awakening.

Scissors: Are you cutting someone out of your life through a separation? Don't use words that inflict wounds or hurt the feelings of others.

Scorpion: Stinging remarks may cause you a lot of problems.

Seesaw: You may be having a contest or struggle with who will be in the lead. Perhaps it is more appropriate to alternate between the two of you and share the responsibility.

Shark: A voracious predator who threatens you. Be careful who you associate with at this time, as a crafty person may prey upon you through trickery.

Sheep: Your approach may be trusting, timid, and bashful. Be careful, your innocence could leave you defenseless and abused.

Shell: You are wearing an external covering for protection. It is time for more exposure and adventure. Come out of that shell.

Skeleton: Are you being supported by those around you? Is your life so structured that you have no flexibility?

Snail: If you are slow-moving and sluggish now, perhaps the universe is telling you to relax and take it easy.

Snake: Phallic symbol. Snakes should not be feared, as they represent the silent, sensuous movement within you, awakening your spiritual power and unleashing unlimited potential.

Stairs: Become more aware of your rise in power and status.

Stork: A messenger, who brings news of a new beginning. The birth of something.

Suitcase: Go ahead, pack up your troubles and leave them behind. Smile! It's contagious.

Sun: The Sun is the symbol of life, the giver of light, power, and energy.

Swan: You can gracefully glide over an emotional issue. Good luck.

Sword: Take swift action and rise above the situation. Use the sword to cut out the deadwood in your life.

T

Table: Get ready, there are many people coming to your house for dinner.

Tail: You are finishing off something, bringing up the tail end. The worst is behind you.

Tears: Releasing emotional blocks or feelings which have been suppressed.

Teddy Bear: Snuggle up to something that is warm, affectionate, and loving.

Teeth: You are giving something new form. Chewing or tearing it down for easier digestion.

Telephone: A message from a long distance. Transmission from another place in time.

Tent: You may reside somewhere for a short period of time. Take the time to build a solid foundation in your life.

Toilet: A time in your life for releasing and letting go of unwanted things.

Tornado: There are changes that must be made suddenly. You will not have an opportunity to get centered and balanced, this one may catch you off-guard. Don't be afraid, swift action is sometimes better.

Train: Your vulnerability can cause you to be lead by someone with tremendous power. Follow this person's train of thought. This is a favorable journey.

Tree: A tree is symbolic of you as a person. The roots are your foundation, and the subconscious mind. The trunk is the conscious mind and the branches are the superconsciousness. If there are many branches and leaves, then your intellect is very strong. Examine which part of the tree seems to be emphasized.

Triangle: You will experience an easy flow with the least amount of resistance. Pulling together all of your talents in a business proposition.

Tunnel: Go with the flow, don't be afraid to try something new. This may be an entrance into the unknown.

Turtle: Your drive and determination are very important. You are the one who will accomplish many things. Protect yourself in the process.

U

Umbilical Cord: Use the knowledge that you are fed from the astral plane, which nurtures and sustains you. The cord that connects you with your astral body, so go ahead and travel wherever you desire.

Umbrella: A protective cover from an emotional upset. Stay out of the storm that is brewing.

V

Vase: A gift cup of flowers or something pleasant is coming your way.

Violin: Are you fiddling around and accomplishing very little?

Volcano: Explosive upheavals of anger and animosity will cause trouble. It is important to release the anger, but through a good physical workout, or a long walk, something that allows you to vent the steam.

W

Wagon: A heavy burden that you are carrying around; can be difficult if you don't have the energy to support all that is happening.

Waterfall: You are receiving an abundance of credit and recognition for your work. Release and let go in a positive way.

Wave: The trauma continues to exist until you resolve the issue. Release this powerful emotion.

Web: Don't get trapped or caught in your own creation.

Well: Focus on your wish and it will manifest. Be sure you get to the bottom of things.

Whale: You have a "whale" of a good venture coming soon. Use your intuition as your guide.

Wheel: See circle.

Whip: There is hostility directed through a superior who rides over you. Sexual aggressiveness, pleasure and pain at the same time.

Window: You're seeing things clearly. Seeing beyond your normal range. Explore the new horizons.

Wings: Rise above all obstacles with renewed freedom.

Witch: Someone may be instilling fears in you, through unconscious control. This power is manipulative.

Y

Yarn: Are you telling "yarns"? Are you wondering if a current issue will ever end?

Yod: The finger of God pointing in your direction. Inspiration that is given to you like little gentle drops of falling rain.

Yoke: Strapped down by your attitudes and beliefs can be difficult to carry around. Don't let yourself be dominated by other people.

Yo-yo: You are repeating the same lessons over and over again. Stop, unwind, and concentrate on your experiences.

Z

Zebra: There is a tremendous amount of energy that is being directed toward you. There are mixed feeling, one cannot be sure if it is positive or negative.

☾ REACH FOR THE MOON

Llewellyn publishes hundreds of books on your favorite subjects!
To get these exciting books, including those on the following pages, check your
local bookstore or order them directly from Llewellyn.

Order by Phone
- Call toll-free within the U.S. and Canada, 1-877-NEW-WRLD
- In Minnesota, call (651) 291-1970
- We accept VISA, MasterCard, and American Express

Order by Mail
- Send the full price of your order (MN residents add 7% sales tax)
  in U.S. funds, plus postage & handling to:
  Llewellyn Worldwide
  P.O. Box 64383, Dept. K813-3
  St. Paul, MN 55164–0383, U.S.A.

Postage & Handling
- **Standard** (U.S., Mexico, & Canada). If your order is:
  $20.00 or under, add $5.00; $20.01–$100.00, add $6.00
  Over $100, shipping is free
(Continental U.S. orders ship UPS. AK, HI, PR, & P.O. Boxes ship USPS 1st class. Mex. & Can. ship PMB.)
- **Second Day Air** (Continental U.S. only): $10.00 for one book +
  $1.00 per each additional book
- **Express** (AK, HI, & PR only) [Not available for P.O. Box delivery.
  For street address delivery only.]: $15.00 for one book + $1.00 per
  each additional book
- **International Surface Mail:** Add $1.00 per item
- **International Airmail:** Books—Add the retail price of each item;
  Non-book items—Add $5.00 per item

Please allow 4–6 weeks for delivery on all orders.
Postage and handling rates subject to change.

Discounts
We offer a 20% discount to group leaders or agents. You must order a min-
imum of 5 copies of the same book to get our special quantity price.

Visit our website at www.llewellyn.com for more information.

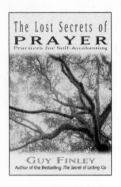

The Lost Secrets of Prayer
Practices for Self Awakening

Guy Finley

Do your prayers go unanswered? Or when they are answered, do the results bring you only temporary relief or happiness? If so, you may be surprised to learn that there are actually two kinds of prayer, and the kind that most of us practice is actually the least effective.

Best-selling author Guy Finley presents *The Lost Secrets of Prayer*, a guide to the second kind of prayer. The purpose of true prayer, as revealed in the powerful insights that make up this book, is not to appeal for what you think you want. Rather, it is to bring you to the point where you are no longer blocked from seeing that everything you need is already here. When you begin praying in this new way, you will discover a higher awareness of your present self. Use these age-old yet forgotten practices for self-awakening and your life will never be the same.

1-56718-276-3, 5¼ x 8, 240 pp. $9.95

The Art of Spritual Healing

Keith Sherwood

Each of you has the potential to be a healer; to heal yourself and to become a channel for healing others. Healing energy is always flowing through you. Learn how to recognize and tap this incredible energy source. You do not need to be a victim of disease or poor health. Rid yourself of negativity and become a channel for positive healing.

Become acquainted with your three auras and learn how to recognize problems and heal them on a higher level before they become manifested in the physical body as disease.

Special techniques make this book a "breakthrough" to healing power, but you are also given a concise, easy-to-follow regimen of good health to follow in order to maintain a superior state of being. This is a practical guide to healing.

0-87542-720-0, 224 pp., 5 ¼ x 8, illus. $9.95

The Magical Power of the Saints
Evocation and Candle Rituals

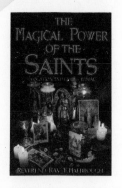

Reverend Ray T. Malbrough

Throughout the ancient world, people presented offerings to the deities along with petitions and prayers. Most often they were supplicated with a bonfire or flame from an oil lamp.

In time, Christianity pushed the ancestral deities into the background. Within the religious systems of Santeria, Condomble and Voudun, people began to worship their gods under the guise of Christian saints. The saints took on characteristics of the pagan deities. They had assigned to them special days of the week, a candle of a particular color, and rulership over certain problems and occupations. This belief in the saint's ability to intercede on the petitioner's behalf continues to this day.

In this book, you will find a guide to 74 saints and their attributes. Learn how to evoke the saints for practical help in your life through prayer, candle burning, and divination.

1-56718-456-1, 240 pp., 5³⁄₁₆ x 8, illus.   **$7.95**